L'Estrange Surname

Ireland: 1600s to 1900s

From Ireland Church Records of Baptism, Marriage and Death

Comprised of Roman Catholic and Church of Ireland Records

From Counties Carlow, Cork, Kerry and Dublin City

Compiled by **Donovan Hurst**

February 20, 2013

Dedication

This work is dedicated to all of those that came before us and shaped our lives to make us the people that we are today.

Table of Contents

Introduction

This is a compilation of individuals who have the surname of L'Estrange that lived in the country of Ireland from the 1600s to the 1900s. I have placed each entry into one of four categories: Families, Individual Births/Baptisms, Individual Burials, and Individual Marriages. If a marriage entry primarily concerns an Individual L'Estrange whom is female, then I have placed that entry under the category of Individual Marriages. If a marriage entry primarily concerns an Individual L'Estrange whom is male, then I have placed that entry under the category of Families. Images of many of these listings are available at http://churchrecords.irishgenealogy.ie/churchrecords/.

To help guide the reader of this work, the format of this book is as follows:

- Main Family Entry (Husband and Wife) (Father and Mother)

  - Child of Main Family Entry, including Spouse(s) when available

    - Grandchild of Main Family Entry, including Spouse(s) when available

      - Great-Grandchild of Main Family Entry, including Spouse(s) when available

(Bolded Text) following any entry includes any additional information such as Residence(s), Occupation(s), Signature(s), etc. when available.

Hurst

Some of the fonts used in this work symbolizes Celtic writing. The traditional letters, numbers, and punctuation marks and their Celtic counterparts are as follows:

Traditional Letters (Uppercase & Lowercase)

A a B b C c D d E f G g H h I i J j K k L l M m N n O o P p Q q R r S s T t U u V v W w X x Y y Z z

Celtic Letters (Uppercase & Lowercase)

A a B b C c D ð E e F ꝼ G g H h I í J j K k L l M m

N n O o P p Q q R ʀ S s T t U u V ʋ W ɯ X x Y y Z z

Traditional Numbers

1 2 3 4 5 6 7 8 9 10

Celtic Numbers

1 2 3 4 5 6 7 8 9 10

Traditional Punctuation

. , : ' " & - ( )

Celtic Punctuation

. , : ' " & - ( )

Parish Churches

Carlow (Church of Ireland)

Carlow Parish.

Cork & Ross

(Roman Catholic or RC)

Schull East Parish.

Dublin (Church of Ireland)

Arbour Hill Barracks Parish, Clontarf Parish, Irishtown Parish, Leeson Park Parish, Rathmines Parish, Sandford Parish, St. Anne Parish, St. Audoen Parish, St. Bride Parish, St. Catherine Parish, St. George Parish, St. James Parish, St. John Parish, St. Mark Parish, St. Mary Parish, St. Michan Parish, St. Nicholas Without Parish, St. Paul Parish, St. Peter Parish, St. Stephen Parish, St. Thomas Parish, and St. Werburgh Parish.

Dublin (Roman Catholic or RC)

Chapelizod Parish, Harrington Street Parish, Rathfarnham Parish, Rathmines Parish, SS. Michael & John Parish, St. Agatha Parish, St. Andrew Parish, St. Audoen Parish, St. Catherine Parish, St. James Parish, St. Lawrence Parish, St. Mary Parish, St. Mary, Pro Cathedral Parish, St. Michan Parish, and St. Nicholas Parish.

Families

- Alfred L'Estrange & Julie McGuinness

  o Josephine Frances L'Estrange – b. 1885, bapt. 1885 (Baptism, St. Andrew Parish (RC))

Alfred L'Estrange (father):

Residence - 13 Poolbeg Street - 1885

- Andrew L'Estrange & Jane Unknown

  o Catherine L'Estrange – bapt. 1792 (Baptism, St. Andrew Parish (RC))

  o Eleanor L'Estrange – bapt. 1793 (Baptism, St. Andrew Parish (RC))

  o Christopher L'Estrange – b. 1794 (Baptism, St. Andrew Parish (RC))

- Anthony L'Estrange, b. 1759, d. 3 Dec 1813 (Burial, St. Anne Parish) & Anne L'Estrange, bur. aft. 3 Dec 1813 (Burial, St. Anne Parish)

Anthony L'Estrange (husband):

Age at Death - 54 years

- Anthony L'Estrange & Margaret Unknown

  o Edward L'Estrange – bapt. 30 May 1791 (Baptism, St. Werburgh Parish)

  o George L'Estrange – b. Oct 1793, bur. 8 Oct 1793 (Burial, St. Werburgh Parish)

George L'Estrange (son):

Residence - Dame Street - before October 8, 1793

Age at Death - one week

Hurst

- ○ John L'Estrange – bapt. 19 Oct 1796 (Baptism, **St. Werburgh Parish**), bur. 25 Jun 1802 (Burial, **St. Werburgh Parish**)

John L'Estrange (son):

Residence - Dame Street - before June 25, 1802

Age at Death - 5 years

- ○ Francis L'Estrange – bapt. 19 Jul 1802 (Baptism, **St. Werburgh Parish**)

Anthony L'Estrange (father):

Residence - Arran Street - May 30, 1791

Dame Street - October 19, 1796

July 19, 1802

- • Anthony L'Estrange & Mary Taylor – 12 Dec 1839 (Marriage, **St. Peter Parish**)

Anthony L'Estrange (husband):

Residence - Leeson Street - December 12, 1839

Mary Taylor (wife):

Residence - Leeson Street - December 12, 1839

Occupation - Spinster - December 12, 1839

Wedding Witnesses:

Thomas Ruprolds & John Phibbs

L'Estrange Surname Ireland: 1600s to 1900s

- Benjamin L'Estrange & Augustina L'Estrange

  o Louisa Florence L'Estrange – bapt. 6 Aug 1865 (Baptism, **Arbour Hill Barracks Parish**)

Benjamin L'Estrange (father):

Residence - Island Bridge Barracks - August 6, 1865

Occupation - Corporal, 10th Hussars - August 6, 1865

- Charles L'Estrange & Margaret L'Estrange

  o Robert L'Estrange – bapt. 11 Sep 1768 (Baptism, **St. Mark Parish**)

  o Jane L'Estrange – bapt. 9 Sep 1770 (Baptism, **St. Mark Parish**)

  o Mary L'Estrange – bapt. 18 Feb 1776 (Baptism, **St. Mark Parish**)

  o Charles L'Estrange – bapt. 28 Jan 1778 (Baptism, **St. Mark Parish**)

  o John L'Estrange – bapt. 19 Jan 1780 (Baptism, **St. Mark Parish**)

  o William L'Estrange – bapt. 29 Feb 1784 (Baptism, **St. Mark Parish**)

  o Elizabeth L'Estrange – bapt. 9 Jul 1786 (Baptism, **St. Mark Parish**)

Charles L'Estrange (father):

Residence - Poolbeg Street - September 11, 1768

January 19, 1780

February 29, 1784

July 9, 1786

White's Quay - September 9, 1770

Hawkins Street - February 18, 1776

Hurst

January 28, 1778

- Christopher L'Estrange & Alice L'Estrange

  - Frances Alice L'Estrange – bapt. 6 Dec 1832 (Baptism, **St. Mary Parish**)

Christopher L'Estrange (father):

Residence - 59 Sackville Street - December 6, 1832

Occupation - Gentleman - December 6, 1832

- Christopher L'Estrange & Anne O'Toole – 30 Mar 1851 (Marriage, **St. Mary, Pro Cathedral Parish (RC)**)

Wedding Witnesses:

John Keogh & William Leonard

- Christopher L'Estrange & Jane L'Estrange

  - Henry L'Estrange – b. 1810, bapt. 14 Feb 1810 (Baptism, **St. George Parish**)

- Christopher Carleton L'Estrange & Unknown

Signature:

  - Jane L'Estrange & William Orme (O r m e) – 10 Oct 1837 (Marriage, **St. Peter Parish**)

L'Estrange Surname Ireland: 1600s to 1900s

Jane L'Estrange (daughter):

Residence - Fitzwilliam Square - October 10, 1837

Occupation - Spinster - October 10, 1837

William Orme (son-in-law):

Residence - Millbrook, Moygownagh Parish, Co. Mayo - October 10, 1837

Wedding Witnesses:

Christopher Carleton L'Estrange & R. La Touche

o   Louisa L'Estrange & William Digges La Touche – 13 Sep 1842 (Marriage, **St. Peter Parish**)

Louisa L'Estrange (daughter):

Residence - 9 Fitzwilliam Square West - September 13, 1842

Occupation - Spinster - September 13, 1842

William Digges La Touche (son-in-law):

Residence - 2 Fitzwilliam Square East - September 13, 1842

Occupation - Esquire - September 13, 1842

Wedding Witnesses:

Christopher Carleton L'Estrange & R. D. La Touche

o   Sidney Frances L'Estrange & Robert Orme (O r m e) – 16 May 1843 (Marriage, **St. Peter Parish**)

Sidney Frances L'Estrange (daughter):

Residence - 9 Fitzwilliam Square - May 16, 1843

Hurst

Robert Orme (son-in-law):

Residence - 11 Pembroke Road - May 16, 1843

Occupation - Esquire - May 16, 1843

Wedding Witnesses:

Gr. Naughen Jackson & Christopher Carleton L'Estrange

- o   Mary L'Estrange & John George – 10 Aug 1848 (Marriage, **St. Peter Parish**)

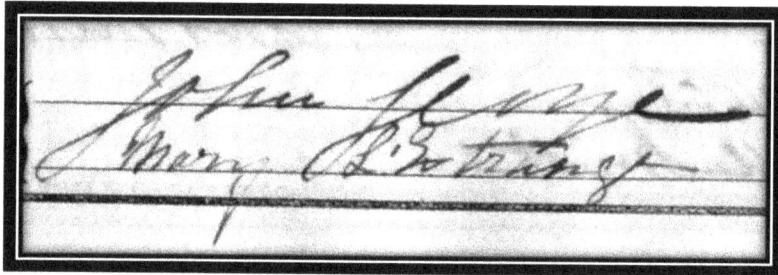

Signatures:

Mary L'Estrange (daughter):

Residence - Fitzwilliam Square - August 10, 1848

John George, son of John George (son-in-law):

Residence - Fitzwilliam Square - August 10, 1848

Occupation - Barrister at Law - August 10, 1848

Relationship Status at Marriage - widow

John George (father):

Occupation - Merchant

L'Estrange Surname Ireland: 1600s to 1900s

Christopher Carleton L'Estrange (father):

Occupation - Major in Militia

Wedding Witnesses:

Christopher Carleton L'Estrange & J. Clarkson

Signatures:

- Collin L'Estrange & Grace L'Estrange
  - Jane L'Estrange & Alexander Perceval – 11 Feb 1808 (Marriage, **St. George Parish**)

Jane L'Estrange (daughter):

Residence - St. George Parish & Moyston, King's County - February 11, 1808

Alexander Perceval (son-in-law):

Residence - St. George Parish & Temple House, Co. Sligo - February 11, 1808

Occupation - Esquire - February 11, 1808

- Daniel L'Estrange & Judith Larkin
  - Daniel Marcy L'Estrange – bapt. Apr 1823 (Baptism, **St. Nicholas Parish** (RC))
  - Anne L'Estrange – bapt. 2 Nov 1825 (Baptism, **St. Nicholas Parish** (RC))
  - Gulielmo L'Estrange – bapt. Oct 1827 (Baptism, **St. Nicholas Parish** (RC))
  - James L'Estrange – bapt. 29 Jun 1831 (Baptism, **SS. Michael & John Parish** (RC))

Hurst

- Daniel L'Estrange & Julianne L'Estrange

  o Anne L'Estrange & James O'Coughan – 24 Nov 1856 (Marriage, **St. Mary, Pro Cathedral Parish (RC)**)

Anne L'Estrange (daughter):

Residence - **25 Little Mary Street** - November 24, 1856

James O'Coughan, son of Thomas O'Coughan & Elizabeth O'Coughan (son-in-law):

Residence - **11 Little Mary Street** - November 24, 1856

Wedding Witnesses:

James Laley & Elizabeth Mulhall

- Daniel L'Estrange & Margaret Kelly

  o Christopher Joseph L'Estrange – b. 18 Dec 1897, bapt. 20 Dec 1897 (Baptism, **SS. Michael & John Parish (RC)**)

Daniel L'Estrange (father):

Residence - **49 South Great George's Street** - December 20, 1897

- Daniel L'Estrange & Mary Hanbidge – 10 Feb 1850 (Marriage, **St. Andrew Parish (RC)**)

  o Daniel L'Estrange – bapt. 1851 (Baptism, **St. Andrew Parish (RC)**)

  o Jane L'Estrange – bapt. 1852 (Baptism, **St. Andrew Parish (RC)**)

  o Catherine L'Estrange – bapt. 1854 (Baptism, **St. Andrew Parish (RC)**)

  o Mary Teresa L'Estrange – bapt. 1857 (Baptism, **St. Andrew Parish (RC)**)

  o John Patrick L'Estrange – b. 1858, bapt. 1858 (Baptism, **St. Andrew Parish (RC)**)

L'Estrange Surname Ireland: 1600s to 1900s

Daniel L'Estrange (father):

    Residence - 3 Castle Market - 1858

Wedding Witnesses:

James Dunne & Elizabeth Hanbidge

- Edmond L'Estrange & Anne Unknown

  o Elizabeth Frances L'Estrange – bapt. 24 Feb 1802 (Baptism, St. Werburgh Parish)

Edmond L'Estrange (father):

    Residence - Portobello Barracks - February 24, 1802

- Edmond L'Estrange & Unknown

  o Harriet Georgina L'Estrange & John Henry Cole Wynne – 12 Sep 1861 (Marriage, St. Peter Parish)

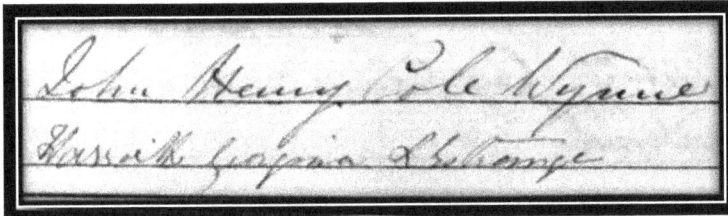

Signatures:

Harriet Georgina L'Estrange (daughter):

    Residence - 3 Mount Street, Crescent - September 12, 1861

John Henry Cole Wynne, son of Owen Wynne (son-in-law):

    Residence - Ardaghowen, Sligo - September 12, 1861

    Occupation - Esquire - September 12, 1861

Hurst

Owen Wynne (father):

    Occupation - Esquire

Edmond L'Estrange (father):

    Occupation - Esquire

Wedding Witnesses:

William Palliser & Constance A. L'Estrange

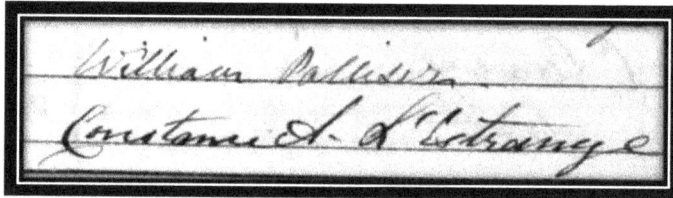

Signatures:

- Edward L'Estrange & Julia McMahon
  - Edward L'Estrange – bapt. 1833 (Baptism, **St. Andrew Parish** (RC))
  - Margaret L'Estrange – bapt. 13 Jun 1834 (Baptism, **St. Catherine Parish** (RC))
  - Josephine Georgina L'Estrange – b. 1 Jun 1834, bapt. 1 Feb 1835 (Baptism, **St. Peter Parish**)
  - Adelaide Victoria L'Estrange – b. 29 Feb 1836, bapt. 11 Oct 1837 (Baptism, **St. Mark Parish**)
  - Elizabeth L'Estrange – bapt. 1836 (Baptism, **St. Andrew Parish** (RC))

Edward L'Estrange (father):

    Residence - 5 Church Lane - February 1, 1835

        122 Townsend Street - October 11, 1837

    Occupation - Soldier - October 11, 1837

L'Estrange Surname Ireland: 1600s to 1900s

- Edward T. L'Estrange & Mary Joan Crawley

  o John Mary L'Estrange – b. 4 May 1884, bapt. 9 May 1884 (Baptism, **St. Agatha Parish (RC)**)

  o Edward Mary L'Estrange – b. 30 Jun 1886, bapt. 6 Jul 1886 (Baptism, **St. Agatha Parish (RC)**)

Edward L'Estrange (father):

Residence - 10 St. Clare's Terrace - May 9, 1884

20 Clonliffe Avenue - July 6, 1886

- Francis L'Estrange & Anne Unknown

  o Elizabeth Augusta Jane L'Estrange – b. 28 Feb 1816, bapt. 26 Mar 1816 (Baptism, **St. Peter Parish**)

- Francis L'Estrange & Catherine Elizabeth Mathews – 20 Mar 1830 (Marriage, **St. Peter Parish**)

Signature:

  o Catherine Margaret L'Estrange & William Sheffield Harding – 8 Aug 1860 (Marriage, **St. Peter Parish**)

Signatures:

Hurst

Catherine Margaret L'Estrange (daughter):

    Residence - Landour, Raglan Road - August 8, 1860

William Sheffield Harding, son of William Henry Harding (son-in-law):

    Residence - 16 Upper Buckingham Street - August 8, 1860

    Occupation - Lieutenant in the 2nd Battalion, 22nd Regiment - August 8, 1860

William Henry Harding (father):

    Occupation - Barrister

Francis L'Estrange (father):

    Occupation - Doctor of Medicine

Wedding Witnesses:

Francis L'Estrange & Edward Mathews

Signatures:

L'Estrange Surname Ireland: 1600s to 1900s

o   Edward Napoleon L'Estrange & Belinda Emily Bomford – 2 Apr 1878 (Marriage, **St. Stephen Parish**)

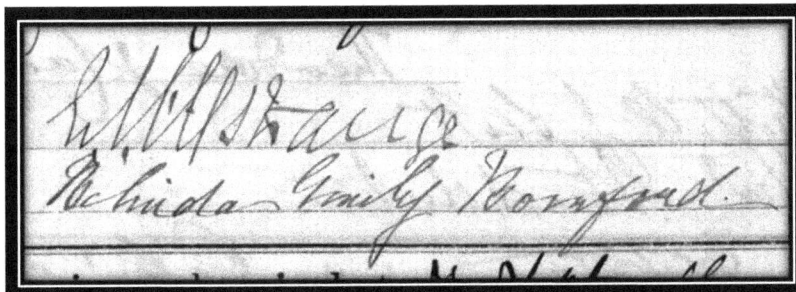

Signatures:

■ Edward Bomford L'Estrange – b. 20 Feb 1882, bapt. 23 Mar 1882 (Baptism, **St. Stephen Parish**)

Edward Napoleon L'Estrange (son):

Residence - Landore, Raglan Road - April 2, 1878

37 Lower Baggot Street - March 23, 1882

Occupation - Major, Royal Scots Fusiliers - April 2, 1878

Relationship Status at Marriage - widow

Belinda Emily Bomford, daughter of Isaac North Bomford (daughter-in-law):

Residence - 29 Upper Fitzwilliam Street - April 2, 1878

Isaac North Bomford (father):

Occupation - Esquire

Francis L'Estrange (father):

Occupation - Medical Doctor

Hurst

Wedding Witnesses:

B. S. Whitney & H. Bomford

Signatures:

Francis L'Estrange (father):

Residence - Dawson Street, St. Anne Parish - March 20, 1830

Catherine Elizabeth Mathews (mother):

Residence - Charlemont Place - March 20, 1830

Wedding Witnesses:

Edward Mathews & James Rainsford

- Francis L'Estrange & Mabella Saunderson – 29 Jul 1727 (Marriage, **St. Mary Parish**)

Francis L'Estrange (husband):

Occupation - Captain - July 29, 1727

- Francis L'Estrange & Mary Anne Dunlop – 7 Sep 1844 (Marriage, **St. Peter Parish**)
  - Cecilia Jane Elizabeth L'Estrange – b. 10 Sep 1845, bapt. 8 Oct 1845 (Baptism, **St. Peter Parish**)

Francis L'Estrange (father):

Residence - Keoltown, Westmeath - September 7, 1844

L'Estrange Surname Ireland: 1600s to 1900s

Keoltown, Mulligar - October 8, 1845

Occupation - Esquire - September 7, 1844

Gentleman - October 8, 1845

Mary Anne Dunlop (mother):

Residence - 88 Lower Mount Street - September 7, 1844

Occupation - Spinster - September 7, 1844

Wedding Witnesses:

Thomas J. Kelly & John Swift

- Frederick L'Estrange & Frances Amelia Mathews – 4 May 1829 (Marriage, St. Peter Parish)
  - Margaret Anne L'Estrange & George Beebe – 10 Nov 1857 (Marriage, St. Peter Parish)

Signatures:

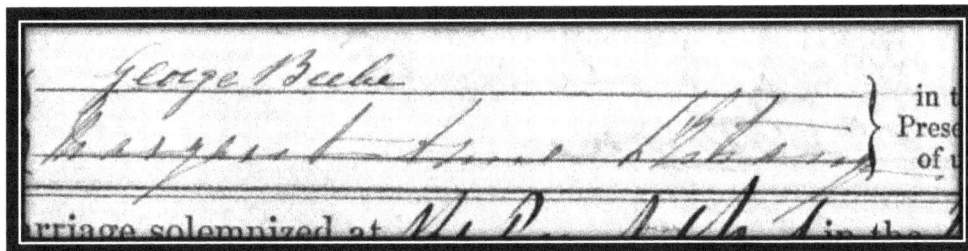

Margaret Anne L'Estrange (daughter):

Residence - 15 Belgrave Road - November 10, 1857

George Beebe, son of William Beebe (son-in-law):

Residence - 26 Upper Mount Pleasant Avenue - November 10, 1857

Occupation - Esquire - November 10, 1857

Hurst

William Beebe (father):

Occupation - Esquire

Frederick L'Estrange (father):

Occupation - Solicitor

Wedding Witnesses:

Frederick L'Estrange & Francis Adolphus L'Estrange

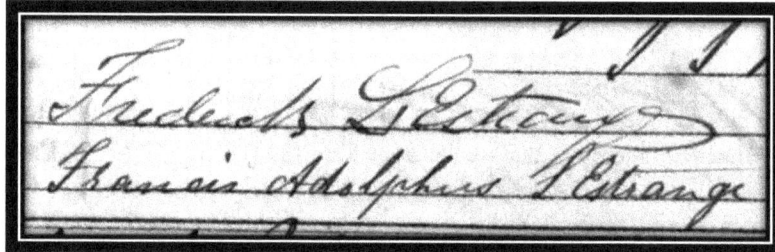

Signatures:

- ○ Albert Halahan L'Estrange, b. 8 Oct 1844, bapt. 28 Oct 1844 (Baptism, **St. Stephen Parish**) & Martha Elizabeth Taylor – 10 Feb 1886 (Marriage, **Sandford Parish**)
  - ▪ Frederick Henry Paget L'Estrange – b. 1888, bapt. 1888 (Baptism, **Sandford Parish**)
  - ▪ Francis Albert L'Estrange – b. 1889, bapt. 1889 (Baptism, **Sandford Parish**)
  - ▪ Henry Rowland L'Estrange – b. 1889, bapt. 1889 (Baptism, **Sandford Parish**)
  - ▪ Albert Cecil Taylor L'Estrange – b. 1891, bapt. 1891 (Baptism, **Sandford Parish**)

Albert Halahan L'Estrange (son):

Residence - Curragh Camp, Co. Kildare - February 10, 1886

Harry Villa, Eglinton Road - 1888

1889

L'Estrange Surname Ireland: 1600s to 1900s

1891

Occupation - Surgeon Major A M Staff - February 10, 1886

Surgeon Major - 1888

1889

Surgeon Major A. M. D. - 1891

Martha Elizabeth Taylor, daughter of Henry Alexander Taylor (daughter-in-law):

Residence - Harryville, Eglinton Road - February 10, 1886

Henry Alexander Taylor (father):

Occupation - Gentleman

Frederick L'Estrange (father):

Occupation - Royal Navy

Wedding Witnesses:

Thomas William Taylor & M. Gibbon

Frederick L'Estrange (father):

Residence - 15 Peter Street, St. Bridget Parish - May 4, 1829

108 Baggot Street - October 28, 1844

Occupation - Attorney at Law - October 28, 1844

Frances Amelia Mathews (mother):

Residence - 8 Charlemont Place - May 4, 1829

Hurst

Wedding Witnesses:

John Mathews & Francis Tynele

- George L'Estrange & Elizabeth Desbrisay – 9 Apr 1755 (Marriage, **St. Michan Parish**)

George L'Estrange (husband):

Occupation - Merchant - April 9 1755

- George L'Estrange & Ellen McNamara
  - Anne L'Estrange – b. 1898, bapt. 1898 (Baptism, **St. Andrew Parish** (RC))

George L'Estrange (father):

Residence - Holles Street Hospital - 1898

- George Henry L'Estrange & Augusta Caroline L'Estrange
  - Henry George L'Estrange – b. 7 Sep 1855, bapt. 5 Oct 1855 (Baptism, **St. Peter Parish**)

George Henry L'Estrange (father):

Residence - 42 Upper Mount Street - October 5, 1855

Occupation - Esquire - October 5, 1855

L'Estrange Surname Ireland: 1600s to 1900s

- George L'Estrange & Unknown

  o Selina Mary L'Estrange, b. 1834 & Hugh Hamilton, b. 1828 – 25 Apr 1853 (Marriage, **St. Werburgh**

  Parish)

Signatures:

Selina Mary L'Estrange (daughter):

   Residence - Dublin Castle - April 25, 1853

   Occupation - Lady - April 25, 1853

Hugh Hamilton (son-in-law):

   Residence - Dublin Castle - April 25, 1853

   Occupation - Esquire - April 25, 1853

            Captain in Army, 1st Dragoon Guards - April 25, 1853

George L'Estrange (father):

   Occupation - Chamberlin, Dublin Castle

Hurst

Wedding Witnesses:

George L'Estrange, Roger Montgomery, & St. German

Signatures:

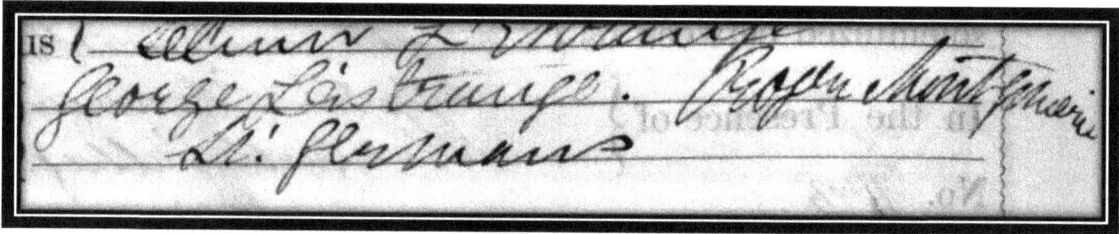

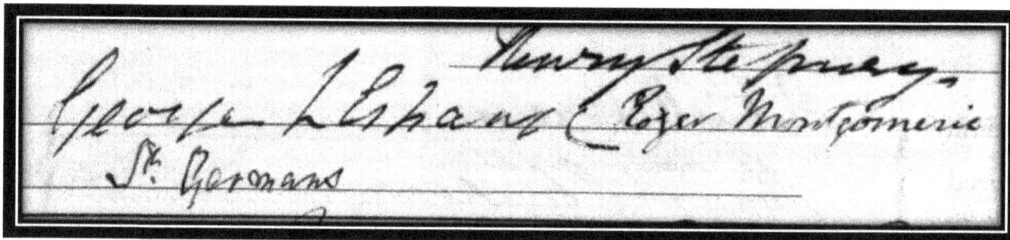

- Gulielmo L'Estrange & Eleanor Unknown

  - Mary L'Estrange – bapt. 1757 (Baptism, **St. Andrew Parish (RC)**)

- Gulielmo L'Estrange & Elizabeth Kirly

  - Gulielmo L'Estrange – b. 29 Apr 1864, bapt. 18 May 1864 (Baptism, **St. Mary, Pro Cathedral Parish (RC)**)

Gulielmo L'Estrange (father):

Residence - 3 McCabe's Street - May 18, 1864

L'Estrange Surname Ireland: 1600s to 1900s

- Gulielmo L'Estrange & Elizabeth L'Estrange

  o Miles L'Estrange (1st Marriage) & Anne Judge – 2 Aug 1863 (Marriage, **St. Mary, Pro Cathedral Parish (RC)**)

    ▪ Mary L'Estrange – b. 25 May 1864, bapt. 30 May 1864 (Baptism, **St. Mary, Pro Cathedral Parish (RC)**)

    ▪ William L'Estrange – b. 29 Aug 1867, bapt. 28 Aug 1867 (Baptism, **St. Agatha Parish (RC)**)

    ▪ Christopher L'Estrange – b. 17 Dec 1869, bapt. 20 Dec 1869 (Baptism, **St. Agatha Parish (RC)**)

    ▪ Elizabeth L'Estrange – b. 13 Oct 1871, bapt. 16 Oct 1871 (Baptism, **St. Agatha Parish (RC)**)

    ▪ Ellen L'Estrange – b. 9 Nov 1874, bapt. 16 Nov 1874 (Baptism, **St. Agatha Parish (RC)**)

  o Miles L'Estrange (2nd Marriage) & Julie Murphy – 9 Jan 1876 (Marriage, **St. Agatha Parish (RC)**)

Miles L'Estrange (son):

Residence - No. 1 Ring's Court - August 2, 1863

20 Beaver Street - May 30, 1864

14 Clarence Street - August 28, 1867

December 20, 1869

October 16, 1871

November 16, 1874

Anne Judge, daughter of Patrick Judge & Ellen Judge (1st wife) (daughter-in-law):

Residence - 1 Cromwell's Court - August 2, 1863

Wedding Witnesses:

John Judge & Ellen Nolan

Hurst

Gulielmo L'Estrange (father):

Residence - 14 Clarence Street - January 9, 1876

Julie Murphy, daughter of John Murphy & Mary Gail (2nd wife) (daughter-in-law):

Residence - 11 Clarence Street - January 9, 1876

Wedding Witnesses:

Terence Cullen & Catherine Ryan

- Gulielmo L'Estrange & Elizabeth Tyrrell – 21 Jan 1759 (Marriage, St. Andrew Parish (RC))

Wedding Witnesses:

John Byrne & Elizabeth Byrne

- Guy Percival L'Estrange & Henrietta Mary L'Estrange

Signature:

- ○ Adelaide Frances L'Estrange & Gregory Sale – 28 Apr 1880 (Marriage, St. George Parish)

Signatures:

L'Estrange Surname Ireland: 1600s to 1900s

Adelaide Frances L'Estrange (daughter):

Residence - 25 Eccles Street, Rathangan, Glebe, Co. Kildare - April 28, 1880

Gregory Sale, son of Samuel Sale (son-in-law):

Residence - Newpark, Naas, Co. Kildare - April 28, 1880

Occupation - Esquire, Medical Doctor - April 28, 1880

Samuel Sale (father):

Occupation - Esquire

Guy Percival L'Estrange (father):

Occupation - Clerk in Holy Orders

Wedding Witnesses:

Guy Percival L'Estrange & Thomas Ridgeway Sale

Signatures:

o   Guy George Edmund L'Estrange – b. 8 Oct 1881, bapt. 12 Apr 1882 (Baptism, **Rathmines Parish**)

Hurst

Guy Percival L'Estrange (father):

Residence - 1 Prince Arthur Terrace - April 12, 1882

Occupation - Clerk in Holy Orders - April 12, 1882

- Henry L'Estrange & Catherine Walsh
  - Vincent Henry L'Estrange – b. 10 Jan 1884, bapt. 14 Jan 1884 (Baptism, **St. Mary, Pro Cathedral Parish (RC)**)

- Henry L'Estrange & Elizabeth Perry – 27 Dec 1799 (Marriage, **St. Mark Parish**)
  - Margaret L'Estrange – bapt. 2 Nov 1800 (Baptism, **St. Mark Parish**)
  - Henry L'Estrange – bapt. 28 Dec 1802 (Baptism, **St. Mark Parish**)
  - Robert L'Estrange – bapt. 24 Mar 1805 (Baptism, **St. Mark Parish**)
  - John L'Estrange – bapt. 17 Apr 1808 (Baptism, **St. Mary Parish**)
  - Elizabeth L'Estrange – bapt. 2 May 1813 (Baptism, **St. Paul Parish**)
  - John Joseph L'Estrange – bapt. 16 Apr 1815 (Baptism, **St. Paul Parish**)

Henry L'Estrange (father):

Residence - George's Street - November 2, 1800

13 Poolbeg Street - December 28, 1802

- Henry L'Estrange & Grace L'Estrange
  - George Burdett L'Estrange – bapt. 15 May 1796 (Baptism, **St. George Parish**)

- Henry L'Estrange & Jane Reardon
  - Henry L'Estrange – bapt. 23 Aug 1829 (Baptism, **SS. Michael & John Parish (RC)**)

- Henry L'Estrange & Mary L'Estrange
  - Elizabeth L'Estrange – bapt. 10 Jan 1753 (Baptism, **St. Audoen Parish**)

L'Estrange Surname Ireland: 1600s to 1900s

- Henry L'Estrange & Mary L'Estrange

  o Anne L'Estrange – bapt. 25 Aug 1827 (Baptism, **St. Mary, Pro Cathedral Parish** (RC))

  o Jane L'Estrange – bapt. 13 Aug 1832 (Baptism, **St. Mary, Pro Cathedral Parish** (RC))

Henry L'Estrange (father):

Residence - Liffey Street - August 25, 1827

- Henry L'Estrange & Mary Unknown

  o Catherine L'Estrange – bapt. 1806 (Baptism, **St. Andrew Parish** (RC))

- Henry P. L'Estrange & Grace Burdett

  o Grace Mary O'Mahony – b. 1818, bapt. 20 Dec 1856 (Baptism, **St. Mary, Pro Cathedral Parish** (RC))

Henry P. L'Estrange (father):

Residence - 38 Upper Rutland Street - December 20, 1856

- Henry P. L'Estrange & Mary Bennett – 17 Feb 1817 (Marriage, **St. Mary Parish**)
- Hilary Frederick L'Estrange & Mary Mulock – 10 May 1831 (Marriage, **St. George Parish**)

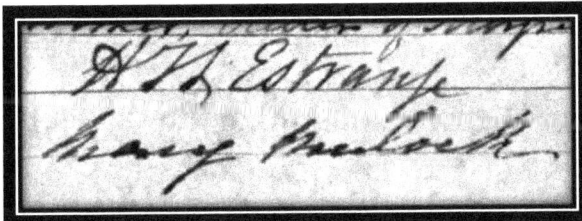

Signatures:

  o Alfred Guy L'Estrange – b. 9 Mar 1832, bapt. 31 May 1832 (Baptism, **St. George Parish**)

Hurst

Hilary Frederick L'Estrange (father):

Residence - No. 17 Fitzwilliam Square South, St. Peter Parish, Dublin - May 10, 1831

May 31, 1832

Occupation - Esquire - May 31, 1832

Mary Mulock (mother):

Residence - No. 24 Gardiner's Place, St. George Parish - May 10, 1831

Wedding Witnesses:

William H. Mulock & Robert Colvile

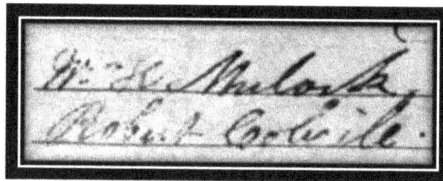

Signatures:

- James L'Estrange & Rose Grahams – 19 Jun 1832 (Marriage, **Chapelizod Parish** (RC))
  - John L'Estrange – bapt. 17 Jun 1836 (Baptism, **St. James Parish** (RC))

Wedding Witnesses:

Michael Scully & Jane L'Estrange

- Jeremiah L'Estrange & Marcella Egan
  - Edward L'Estrange & Mary Egan – 1 Dec 1859 (Marriage, **St. Lawrence Parish** (RC))

Edward L'Estrange (son):

Residence - 40 Guild Street - December 1, 1859

L'Estrange Surname Ireland: 1600s to 1900s

Mary Egan, daughter of Thomas Egan & Sarah Thomas (daughter-in-law):

Residence - 40 Guild Street - December 1, 1859

Wedding Witnesses:

Cornelius Francis Clifford & Patrick Joseph Mann

- John L'Estrange & Catherine Blanch – 15 Sep 1828 (Marriage, **St. Nicholas Parish (RC)**)
  - Catherine L'Estrange – bapt. 17 Nov 1833 (Baptism, **St. James Parish (RC)**)
  - Catherine L'Estrange – bapt. 14 Jan 1836 (Baptism, **St. James Parish (RC)**)
  - Joseph L'Estrange – bapt. 30 Jan 1840 (Baptism, **St. James Parish (RC)**)
  - Catherine L'Estrange – bapt. 31 Jul 1842 (Baptism, **St. James Parish (RC)**)
  - James L'Estrange – bapt. 3 Mar 1844 (Baptism, **St. James Parish (RC)**)
  - Margaret L'Estrange – bapt. 10 Nov 1845 (Baptism, **St. James Parish (RC)**)
  - James L'Estrange – bapt. 17 Dec 1847 (Baptism, **St. James Parish (RC)**)

Wedding Witnesses:

Thomas Blanch & Catherine Blanch

- John L'Estrange & Catherine Dunne
  - Catherine Mary L'Estrange – b. 18 Dec 1861, bapt. 21 Dec 1861 (Baptism, **St. James Parish (RC)**)

John L'Estrange (father):

Residence - 62 James Street - December 21, 1861

- John L'Estrange & Catherine Vaughn
  - Mary L'Estrange – bapt. 30 Aug 1773 (Baptism, **St. Catherine Parish (RC)**)

Hurst

- John L'Estrange & Elizabeth Catherine Ryan – 30 Sep 1844 (Marriage, **St. Mary, Pro Cathedral Parish** (RC))
  - Michael L'Estrange – b. 1857, bapt. 1857 (Baptism, **St. Andrew Parish** (RC))
  - Mary Sarah L'Estrange – b. 1859, bapt. 1859 (Baptism, **St. Andrew Parish** (RC))
  - John Joseph L'Estrange – b. 1861, bapt. 1861 (Baptism, **St. Andrew Parish** (RC))

John L'Estrange (father):

Residence - 5 Dame Court - 1859

13 Dame Court - 1861

Wedding Witnesses:

Patrick Corgran & Sarah Healy

- John L'Estrange & Esther Unknown
  - Mary L'Estrange – bapt. 25 Dec 1776 (Baptism, **St. James Parish** (RC))
- John L'Estrange & Jane Neill – 9 Nov 1788 (Marriage, **St. Catherine Parish** (RC))
  - James L'Estrange – bapt. Jan 1790 (Baptism, **St. Catherine Parish** (RC))

Wedding Witnesses:

Henry Neill & Matthew Moran

- John L'Estrange & Mary Harford
  - Margaret L'Estrange – bapt. 11 Jan 1833 (Baptism, **St. Michan Parish** (RC))
- John L'Estrange & Mary L'Estrange
  - Daniel L'Estrange & Ellen Clifford – 12 Feb 1877 (Marriage, **St. Mary, Pro Cathedral Parish** (RC))

L'Estrange Surname Ireland: 1600s to 1900s

- Patrick Joseph L'Estrange – b. 24 Jul 1878, bapt. 26 Jul 1878 (Baptism, **St. Michan Parish** (RC))

- Mary Bridget L'Estrange – b. 28 Jan 1880, bapt. 4 Feb 1880 (Baptism, **St. Michan Parish** (RC))

- Catherine Teresa L'Estrange – b. 8 Oct 1882, bapt. 11 Oct 1882 (Baptism, **St. Mary, Pro Cathedral Parish** (RC))

- Daniel Joseph L'Estrange – b. 20 Jul 1884, bapt. 25 Jul 1884 (Baptism, **St. Mary, Pro Cathedral Parish** (RC))

- Patrick Michael L'Estrange – b. 27 Sep 1895, bapt. 30 Sep 1895 (Baptism, **SS. Michael & John Parish** (RC))

Daniel L'Estrange (son):

Residence - Cole's Lane - February 12, 1877

5 Linenhall Street - July 26, 1878

2 Lurgan Street - February 4, 1880

48 Capel Street - October 11, 1882

37 Upper Dorset Street - July 25, 1884

49 South Great George's Street - September 30, 1895

Ellen Clifford, daughter of John Clifford & Catherin Unknown (daughter-in-law):

Residence - 133 Upper Abbey - February 12, 1877

Wedding Witnesses:

James Reilly & Mary Donohoe

- John L'Estrange & Mary Unknown
  - Mary L'Estrange & Thomas Ivory – 4 Nov 1862 (Marriage, **St. Andrew Parish** (RC))

Hurst

Mary L'Estrange (daughter):

    Residence - 2 Cottage Place - November 4, 1862

Thomas Ivory, son of John Ivory & Alice Unknown (son-in-law):

    Residence - 2 Cumberland Street - November 4, 1862

Wedding Witnesses:

Michael Gormley & Catherine Walsh

- John L'Estrange & Unknown
  - Elizabeth L'Estrange & Robert Farquhar – 15 Dec 1864 (Marriage, St. Paul Parish)

Signatures:

Elizabeth L'Estrange (daughter):

    Residence - 48 Arbour Hill - December 15, 1864

    Relationship Status at Marriage - minor

Robert Farquhar, son of Robert Farquhar (son-in-law):

    Residence - Royal Barracks - December 15, 1864

    Occupation - Shoeing Smith, Military Train - December 15, 1864

Robert Farquhar (father):

    Occupation - Cabinet Maker

L'Estrange Surname Ireland: 1600s to 1900s

John L'Estrange (father):

Occupation - Farmer

Wedding Witnesses:

Thomas Browning & George Goldsmith

Signatures:

- o Catherine L'Estrange & George Wilton – 3 Nov 1872 (Marriage, St. Paul Parish)

Signatures:

Catherine L'Estrange (daughter):

Residence - 48 Arbor Hill - November 3, 1872

George Wilton, son of George Wilton (son-in-law):

Residence - Royal Barracks - November 3, 1872

Occupation - Sergeant, 1st Royal Dragoons - November 3, 1872

Hurst

George Wilton (father):

    Occupation - Grocer

John L'Estrange (father):

    Residence - Publican

Wedding Witnesses:

William Horton & Marian Horton

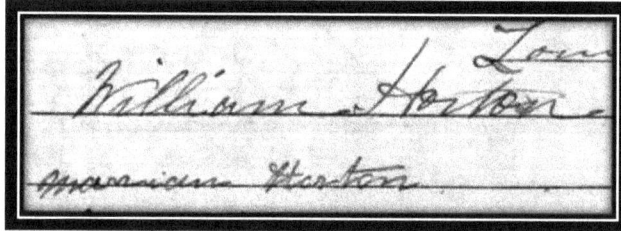

Signatures:

- John L'Estrange & Unknown
  - James L'Estrange & Isabel Best – 22 Nov 1874 (Marriage, St. Audoen Parish (RC))
    - Elizabeth Mary L'Estrange – b. 12 Feb 1877, bapt. 13 Feb 1877 (Baptism, St. Audoen Parish (RC))

James L'Estrange (son):

    Residence - 7 High Street - November 22, 1874

                  February 13, 1877

Isabel Best, daughter of David Best (daughter-in-law):

    Residence - 7 High Street - November 22, 1874

L'Estrange Surname Ireland: 1600s to 1900s

Wedding Witnesses:

John Best & Elizabeth Best

- John Joseph L'Estrange & Margret Anne Ramsen – 24 Oct 1784 (Marriage, **St. Andrew Parish (RC)**)

    o   Joseph L'Estrange – bapt. 1785 (Baptism, **St. Andrew Parish (RC)**)

    o   James L'Estrange – bapt. 1787 (Baptism, **St. Andrew Parish (RC)**)

    o   Mary L'Estrange – bapt. 1787 (Baptism, **St. Andrew Parish (RC)**)

    o   Frances or Francis L'Estrange – bapt. 1788 (Baptism, **St. Andrew Parish (RC)**)

    o   Anthony L'Estrange – bapt. 1790 (Baptism, **St. Andrew Parish (RC)**)

    o   Thomas L'Estrange – bapt. 1795 (Baptism, **St. Andrew Parish (RC)**)

    o   Anne L'Estrange – bapt. 1796 (Baptism, **St. Andrew Parish (RC)**)

    o   Alice L'Estrange – bapt. 1799 (Baptism, **St. Andrew Parish (RC)**)

    o   Mary L'Estrange – bapt. 1799 (Baptism, **St. Andrew Parish (RC)**)

Wedding Witnesses:

Thomas Ramsen & John Corcoran

- Joseph L'Estrange & Delia Callaghan – 15 Apr 1838 (Marriage, **St. Michan Parish (RC)**)

Wedding Witnesses:

George Callaghan & Anne Herbert

- Matthew L'Estrange & Alice Boylan – 23 Sep 1759 (Marriage, **St. Audoen Parish**) (Baptism, **St. Audoen Parish (RC)**)

Wedding Witnesses:

William L'Estrange, Honor L'Estrange, Honor Boylan, & Margaret Conway

Hurst

- Matthew L'Estrange & Margaret Flannigan

  - Mary L'Estrange – b. 1764, bapt. 1764 (Baptism, **SS. Michael & John Parish** (RC))

- Matthew L'Estrange & Margaret Phelan – 3 Apr 1763 (Marriage, **SS. Michael & John Parish** (RC))

  - William L'Estrange – b. 1765, bapt. 1765 (Baptism, **SS. Michael & John Parish** (RC))

  - Mathias L'Estrange – b. 1769, bapt. 1769 (Baptism, **SS. Michael & John Parish** (RC))

  - Michael L'Estrange – bapt. 1771 (Baptism, **SS. Michael & John Parish** (RC))

  - Matthew L'Estrange – bapt. 1774 (Baptism, **SS. Michael & John Parish** (RC))

  - Peter L'Estrange – bapt. 1776 (Baptism, **SS. Michael & John Parish** (RC))

  - Mary L'Estrange – bapt. 1779 (Baptism, **SS. Michael & John Parish** (RC))

Matthew L'Estrange (father):

Residence - Fishamble Street - 1769

Fishamble Street, Harmon's - 1771

Wedding Witnesses:

John Butler & Margaret Phelan

- Matthew L'Estrange & Mary Murphy

  - Mary Anne L'Estrange – bapt. 9 Jan 1820 (Baptism, **St. Audoen Parish** (RC))

  - Michael L'Estrange – bapt. 13 Jan 1822 (Baptism, **SS. Michael & John Parish** (RC))

  - John Francis L'Estrange – bapt. 4 Apr 1824 (Baptism, **SS. Michael & John Parish** (RC))

  - Ellen L'Estrange – b. Dec 1825, bapt. 3 Dec 1825 (Baptism, **St. Audoen Parish** (RC))

  - Margaret L'Estrange – bapt. 4 Nov 1830 (Baptism, **SS. Michael & John Parish** (RC))

L'Estrange Surname Ireland: 1600s to 1900s

- Michael L'Estrange & Catherine Dempsey

  o Jeremiah L'Estrange – bapt. 1772 (Baptism, **SS. Michael & John Parish** (RC))

  o Rose L'Estrange – bapt. 13 May 1782 (Baptism, **St. Audoen Parish** (RC))

Michael L'Estrange (father):

Residence - Michael's Lane - 1772

- Michael L'Estrange & Catherine Fousher – 1840 (Marriage, **St. Nicholas Parish** (RC))

Wedding Witnesses:

Gulielmo Lyons & Margaret L'Estrange

- Michael L'Estrange & Mary Steward – 8 Jun 1794 (Marriage, **St. Andrew Parish** (RC))

  o Matthew L'Estrange – bapt. 26 Jun 1796 (Baptism, **St. Audoen Parish** (RC))

  o Alexander L'Estrange – bapt. 6 Feb 1798 (Baptism, **St. Audoen Parish** (RC))

  o William L'Estrange – bapt. 6 Feb 1798 (Baptism, **St. Audoen Parish** (RC))

Wedding Witnesses:

Thomas Ramjer & Margaret L'Estrange

- Michael L'Estrange & Susan Reilly – 15 Aug 1752 (Marriage, **SS. Michael & John Parish** (RC))

Wedding Witnesses:

William Doran & James Courtney

- Michael L'Estrange & Winifred Poyan – 2 Jun 1759 (Marriage, **St. Catherine Parish** (RC))

Hurst

Wedding Witness:

Pierce Bergin

- N. L'Estrange & Elizabeth Unknown

  - Elizabeth L'Estrange – bapt. 3 Nov 1825 (Baptism, **St. Nicholas Parish** (RC))

- Patrick L'Estrange & Elizabeth Ketro

  - Peter L'Estrange – bapt. 16 Aug 1801 (Baptism, **St. Michan Parish** (RC))

- Peter L'Estrange & Margaret Unknown

  - Mary L'Estrange – bapt. 6 Oct 1802 (Baptism, **St. Audoen Parish** (RC))

- Richard L'Estrange & Anne Byrne (B y r n e)

  - Thomas L'Estrange – bapt. Apr 1811 (Baptism, **St. Catherine Parish** (RC))

  - Barnabas (B a r n a b a s) L'Estrange – bapt. Apr 1811 (Baptism, **St. Catherine Parish** (RC))

- Richard L'Estrange & Margaret Quinn – 29 May 1827 (Marriage, **St. Catherine Parish** (RC))

Wedding Witnesses:

Matthew Reilly & Margaret Connolly

- Robert L'Estrange & Catherine L'Estrange

  - Margaret L'Estrange – bapt. 25 Apr 1744 (Baptism, **St. Mark Parish**)

  - William L'Estrange – bapt. 13 Jul 1746 (Baptism, **St. Mark Parish**)

  - Robert L'Estrange – bapt. 3 Jul 1749 (Baptism, **St. Mark Parish**)

  - Catherine L'Estrange – bapt. 14 Jan 1750 (Baptism, **St. Mark Parish**)

  - Robert L'Estrange – bapt. 16 Jul 1752 (Baptism, **St. Mark Parish**)

L'Estrange Surname Ireland: 1600s to 1900s

Robert L'Estrange (father):

    Residence - Poolbeg Street - April 25, 1744

                          July 13, 1746

                          July 3, 1749

                          January 14, 1750

- Robert L'Estrange & Margaret Garrett
  - Robert L'Estrange – b. 24 Feb 1878, bapt. 8 Mar 1878 (Baptism, **St. Nicholas Parish (RC)**)

Robert L□Estrange (father):

    Residence - 5 Wood Street - March 8, 1878

- Robert Augustus L'Estrange & Elizabeth Mathews – 1 Sep 1819 (Marriage, **St. Peter Parish**)
  - Edgar William L'Estrange, bapt. 29 Nov 1826 (Baptism, **St. Paul Parish**) & Frances Mary Henderson

    – 19 Sep 1855 (Marriage, **St. Peter Parish**)

Signature:

Signatures (Marriage):

Hurst

- Robert Augustus Henry L'Estrange – b. 4 Aug 1858, bapt. 27 Feb 1859 (Baptism, **St. Peter Parish**)

- William Mandeville Ellis L'Estrange – b. 11 Dec 1868, bapt. 25 Jun 1869 (Baptism, **Rathmines Parish**)

- Emily Frances Evangeline L'Estrange – b. 4 Feb 1871, bapt. 2 May 1873 (Baptism, **St. Peter Parish**)

- Edgar Francis Quinlan L'Estrange – b. 12 Sep 1872, bapt. 2 May 1873 (Baptism, **St. Peter Parish**)

- John Henderson L'Estrange & Mary Alice Palmer – 26 Sep 1883 (Marriage, **St. George Parish**)

Signatures:

John Henderson L'Estrange (son):

    Residence - 13 Eccles Street - September 26, 1883

    Occupation - Gentleman - September 26, 1883

    Relationship Status at Marriage - minor

Mary Alice Palmer, daughter of John Palmer (daughter-in-law):

    Residence - 13 Eccles Street - September 26, 1883

L'Estrange Surname Ireland: 1600s to 1900s

John Palmer (father):

Signature:

    Occupation - Gentleman

Edgar William L'Estrange (father):

    Occupation - Solicitor

Wedding Witnesses:

John Palmer & Edgar William L'Estrange

Signatures:

Edgar William L'Estrange (son):

    Residence - 9 Harcourt Terrace - September 19, 1855

        Rathmines - February 27, 1859

        Mount Anthony, Rathmines - June 25, 1869

        Green Mount Milton Road - May 2, 1873

    Occupation - Solicitor - September 19, 1855

Hurst

February 27, 1859

June 25, 1869

May 2, 1873

Frances Mary Henderson, daughter of John Henderson (daughter-in-law):

Residence - Mount Anthony, Rathmines - September 19, 1855

John Henderson (father):

Occupation - Captain in the Army

Robert Augustus L'Estrange (father):

Occupation - Solicitor

Wedding Witnesses:

William Henderson & J. R. Dombrain

Signatures:

Robert Augustus L'Estrange (father):

Residence - St. Anne Parish - September 1, 1819

Elizabeth Mathews (mother):

Residence - St. Peter Parish - September 1, 1819

L'Estrange Surname Ireland: 1600s to 1900s

Wedding Witnesses:

John Mathews & Robert Jager

- Robert Augustus L'Estrange & Unknown
  - Robert Augustus L'Estrange & Isabel Todhunter – 14 Mar 1855 (Marriage, **St. Peter Parish**)

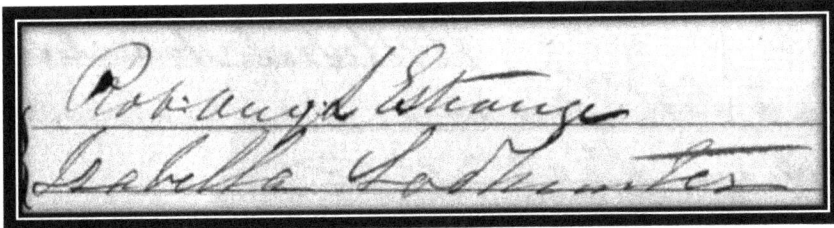

Signatures:

Robert Augustus L'Estrange (son):

    Residence - Arklow - March 14, 1855

    Occupation - Surgeon - March 14, 1855

Isabel Todhunter, daughter of Isaac Todhunter (daughter-in-law):

    Residence - 11 Waterloo Road - March 14, 1855

Isaac Todhunter (father):

    Occupation - Gentleman

Robert Augustus L'Estrange (father):

    Occupation - Solicitor

Wedding Witnesses:

William Todhunter & Edward Billings

Hurst

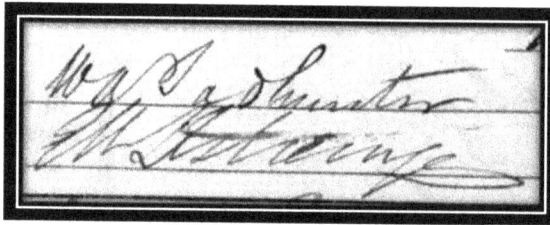

Signatures:

- Robert Augustus L'Estrange & Unknown

  o Augusta Dorothea L'Estrange, b. 1865 & Finlay Monds Finlay Green, b. 1872 – 22 Dec 1897 (Marriage,

    Rathmines Parish)

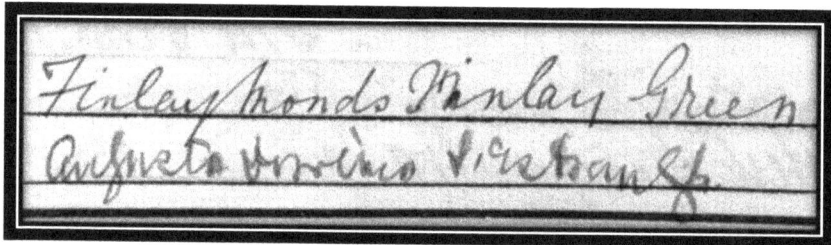

Signatures:

Augusta Dorothea L'Estrange (daughter):

   Residence - 54 Moyne Road, Rathmines - December 22, 1897

   Age at Marriage - 32 years

Finlay Monds Finlay Green, son of Andrew Green (son-in-law):

   Residence - 52 Compton Road, Canonbury, London North - December 22, 1897

   Occupation - Clerk in Holy Orders - December 22, 1897

   Age at Marriage - 25 years

Andrew Green (father):

   Occupation - Land Agent

L'Estrange Surname Ireland: 1600s to 1900s

Robert Augustus L'Estrange (father):

    Occupation - Medical Doctor

Wedding Witnesses:

Leah Adelaide Garner & Marion E. Morton

Signatures:

    ○   Frances L'Estrange & George William Kerr – 28 Dec 1897 (Marriage, **Rathmines Parish**)

Signatures:

Frances L'Estrange (daughter):

    Residence - 54 Moyne Road - December 28, 1897

    Occupation - Gentlewoman - December 28, 1897

George William Kerr, son of Robert S. Kerr (son-in-law).

    Residence - 29 Hargrave Park, London North - December 28, 1897

    Occupation - Clerk in Holy Orders - December 28, 1897

Hurst

Robert S. Kerr (father):

Occupation - Clerk in Holy Orders

Robert Augustus L'Estrange (father):

Occupation - Surgeon

Wedding Witnesses:

Sarah Harris & Marion E. Morton

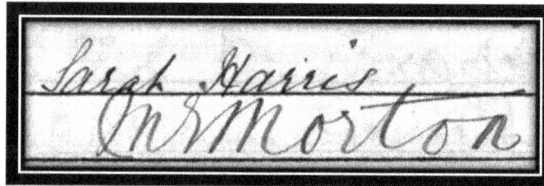

Signatures:

- Samuel L'Estrange & Anne Smith – 4 Dec 1807 (Marriage, **St. Peter Parish**)
- Samuel L'Estrange & Unknown
  - Sarah Frances L'Estrange & Charles Doherty Quinlan – 18 May 1841 (Marriage, **St. Peter Parish**)

Sarah Frances L'Estrange (daughter):

Residence - 7 Adelaide Road - May 18, 1841

Charles Doherty Quinlan (son-in-law):

Residence - Bally Rafter House, Co. Waterford - May 18, 1841

Occupation - Barrister at Law - May 18, 1841

Wedding Witnesses:

Francis Fleming L'Estrange & J. Lock

L'Estrange Surname Ireland: 1600s to 1900s

- o Elizabeth L'Estrange & Charles MacDonnell – 13 Nov 1844 (Marriage, **St. Peter Parish**)

Elizabeth L'Estrange (daughter):

Residence - Adelaide Road - November 13, 1844

Occupation - Spinster - November 13, 1844

Charles MacDonnell (son-in-law):

Residence - Willington, Tallaght Parish - November 13, 1844

Occupation - Reverend Doctor - November 13, 1844

Wedding Witnesses:

Charles Doherty Quinlan & Robert Lucy L'Estrange

- o Francis Fleming L'Estrange & Elizabeth Jane Furey – 30 Aug 1855 (Marriage, **St. Peter Parish**)

Signatures:

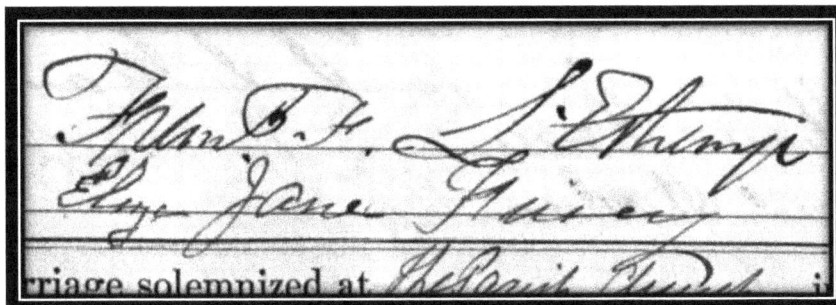

- ▪ Alfred Francis L'Estrange – b. 1850, bapt. 1878 (Baptism, **St. Andrew Parish (RC)**)
- ▪ George Frederick Augustus L'Estrange – b. 23 Jan 1857, bapt. 5 Apr 1857 (Baptism, **St. Peter Parish**)
- ▪ Alfred Francis L'Estrange – b. 17 Apr 1859, bapt. 3 Aug 1859 (Baptism, **St. Peter Parish**)

Hurst

Francis Fleming L'Estrange (father):

Residence - Bloomfield Cottage, South Circular Road - August 30, 1855

78 Lower Mount Street - April 5, 1857

August 3, 1859

1878

Occupation - Esquire - August 30, 1855

April 5, 1857

August 3, 1859

Relationship Status at Marriage - widow

Elizabeth Jane Furey, daughter of George Furey (daughter-in-law):

Residence - 78 Lower Mount Street - August 30, 1855

George Furey (father):

Occupation - Gentleman

Samuel L'Estrange (father):

Occupation - Barrister at Law

Wedding Witnesses:

George John Furey & Charlotte Furey

L'Estrange Surname Ireland: 1600s to 1900s

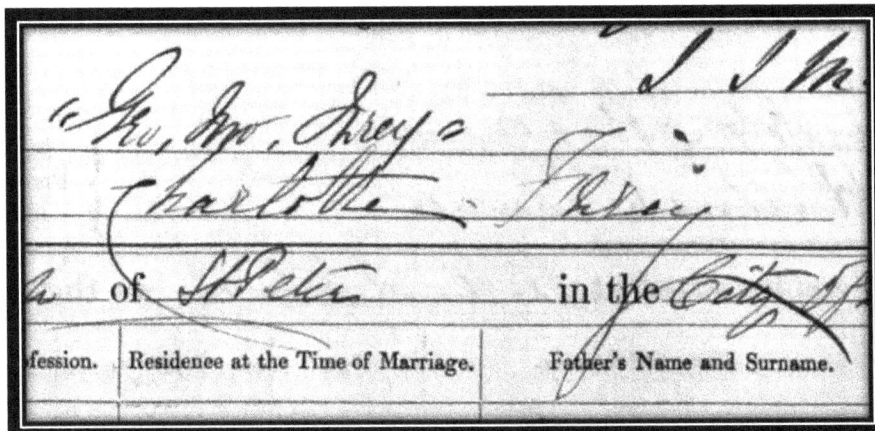

Signatures:

- Thomas L'Estrange & Anne Unknown

  - Margaret L'Estrange & Thomas Nelson – 17 Apr 1901 (Marriage, **St. Mary, Pro Cathedral Parish (RC)**)

Margaret L'Estrange (daughter):

Residence - Woodland, King's County - April 17, 1901

Thomas Nelson, son of James Nelson & Elizabeth Unknown (son-in-law):

Residence - Glasgow - April 17, 1901

Wedding Witnesses:

Edward Unknown & Mary L'Estrange

- Thomas L'Estrange & Elizabeth Unknown

  - Lucy Anne L'Estrange – bapt. 24 Apr 1799 (Baptism, **St. Peter Parish**)

  - George Burrowes L'Estrange – bapt. 3 Jul 1800 (Baptism, **St. Peter Parish**)

Hurst

Thomas L'Estrange (father):

Residence - Mount Pleasant - April 24, 1799

Baggot Street - July 3, 1800

- Thomas L'Estrange & Ellen Hill
  - Mary Jane L'Estrange – b. 1898, bapt. 1898 (Baptism, **St. Andrew Parish (RC)**)
  - Thomas L'Estrange – b. 1901, bapt. 1901 (Baptism, **St. Andrew Parish (RC)**)

Thomas L'Estrange (father):

Residence - Holles Street Hospital - 1898

1901

- Thomas L'Estrange & Frideswide L'Estrange
  - Francis L'Estrange – bapt. 20 Jul 1762 (Baptism, **St. Mary Parish**), bur. 28 Aug 1763 (Burial, **St. Mary Parish**)

Francis L'Estrange (son):

Residence - Jervis Street - before August 28, 1763

- Thomas L'Estrange – b. 25 Apr 1766, bapt. 15 May 1766 (Baptism, **St. Mary Parish**), bur. 16 Mar 1767 (Burial, **St. Mary Parish**)

Thomas L'Estrange (son):

Residence - Jervis Street - before March 16, 1767

- Mabella L'Estrange – b. 12 Aug 1769, bapt. 3 Sep 1769 (Baptism, **St. Mary Parish**)

L'Estrange Surname Ireland: 1600s to 1900s

Thomas L'Estrange (father):

Residence - Jervis Street - May 15, 1766

- Thomas L'Estrange & Jane McKeon

  o Mary L'Estrange – b. 6 Oct 1857, bapt. 8 Oct 1857 (Baptism, **SS. Michael & John Parish (RC)**)

  o Michael L'Estrange – b. 7 Oct 1862, bapt. 10 Oct 1862 (Baptism, **St. Mary, Pro Cathedral Parish (RC)**)

  o Bridget L'Estrange – b. 21 Sep 1863, bapt. 28 Sep 1863 (Baptism, **St. Nicholas Parish (RC)**)

  o Bridget Winifred L'Estrange – b. 4 Nov 1870, bapt. 11 Nov 1870 (Baptism, **St. Nicholas Parish (RC)**)

  o Dennis Patrick L'Estrange – b. 22 Jul 1872, bapt. 29 Jul 1872 (Baptism, **St. Nicholas Parish (RC)**)

  o Thomas L'Estrange – b. 19 Jun 1875, bapt. 24 Jun 1875 (Baptism, **SS. Michael & John Parish (RC)**)

Thomas L'Estrange (father):

Residence - 49 Dame Street - October 8, 1857

30 Great Strand Street - October 10, 1862

6 Bishop Street - September 28, 1863

106 Coombe - November 11, 1870

July 29, 1872

17 Great Longford Street - June 24, 1875

- Thomas L'Estrange & Jane Mealy – 31 Jul 1841 (Marriage, **St. James Parish (RC)**)

  o Margaret L'Estrange – bapt. 11 Aug 1842 (Baptism, **St. James Parish (RC)**)

  o Ellen L'Estrange – bapt. 18 May 1845 (Baptism, **St. James Parish (RC)**)

- ○ Michael L'Estrange – bapt. 13 Apr 1847 (Baptism, **St. James Parish** (RC))

- ○ Mary Jane L'Estrange – bapt. 4 Feb 1849 (Baptism, **St. James Parish** (RC))

- ○ Thomas L'Estrange – bapt. 16 Feb 1852 (Baptism, **St. James Parish** (RC))

- ○ Anne L'Estrange – bapt. 13 Feb 1854 (Baptism, **St. James Parish** (RC))

Wedding Witnesses:

John Molloy & Margaret Mulligan

- Thomas L'Estrange & Margaret Johnstone

  - ○ James L'Estrange – bapt. 30 Jul 1805 (Baptism, **St. Catherine Parish** (RC))

  - ○ Bridget L'Estrange – bapt. 19 Jun 1808 (Baptism, **St. Catherine Parish** (RC))

- Thomas L'Estrange & Susan Egan

  - ○ Frances Catherine L'Estrange – bapt. 23 Jul 1832 (Baptism, **St. Michan Parish** (RC))

- Torriano Francis L'Estrange & Anne Hureda Tomasina L'Estrange

Signature:

- ○ Jane Constance L'Estrange, bapt. 16 Dec 1829 (Baptism, **St. Mary Parish**) & Francis Dickson – 1 Oct 1846 (Marriage, **St. George Parish**)

Signatures:

L'Estrange Surname Ireland: 1600s to 1900s

Jane Constance L'Estrange (daughter):

    Residence - 59 Eccles Street - October 1, 1846

    Occupation - Gentlewoman - October 1, 1846

    Relationship Status at Marriage - minor

Francis Dickson, son of Michael Dickson (son-in-law):

    Residence - Mallingar Parish - October 1, 1846

    Occupation - Captain, 41st Regiment - October 1, 1846

    Relationship Status at Marriage - widow

Michael Dickson (father):

    Occupation - Clergyman

Torriano Francis L'Estrange (father):

    Occupation - Esquire

Wedding Witnesses:

Torriano Francis L'Estrange & John H. Lecky

Signatures:

Hurst

- ○ Thomas L'Estrange & Sarah Garrett – 8 Jun 1850 (Marriage, **St. George Parish**)

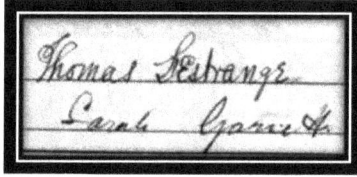

Signatures:

Thomas L'Estrange (father):

Residence - Kilnagama, King's County - June 8, 1850

Occupation - Solicitor - June 8, 1850

Sarah Garrett, daughter of Thomas Garrett (daughter-in-law):

Residence - 17 North Frederick Street - June 8, 1850

Thomas Garrett (father):

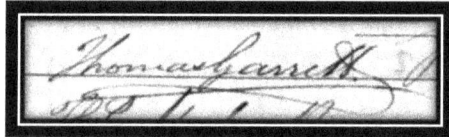

Signature:

Occupation - Solicitor

Torriano Francis L'Estrange (father):

Occupation - Lieutenant in the Army

Wedding Witnesses:

Thomas Garrett & Thomas Mulock

L'Estrange Surname Ireland: 1600s to 1900s

Signatures:

Torriano Francis L'Estrange (father):

    Residence - Upper Dorset Street - December 16, 1829

    Occupation - Halfpay Officer - December 16, 1829

- Unknown L'Estrange & Unknown
  - o   G. W. L'Estrange

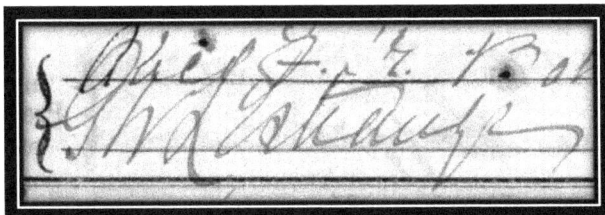

Signature:

- William L'Estrange & Grissell Dunne – 13 Dec 1657 (Marriage, **St. Michan Parish**)

- William L'Estrange & Mary Magrath – 4 Jul 1831 (Marriage, **St. Catherine Parish (RC)**)

Wedding Witnesses:

Patrick Magrath & Mary Halloran

- William L'Estrange & Mary Sweetman – 28 Dec 1777 (Marriage, **St. Audoen Parish**)

William L'Estrange (husband):

    Residence - St. Michael Parish - December 28, 1777

Hurst

Wedding Witnesses:

James Houlin & Matthew L'Estrange

- William L'Estrange & Mary Anne Connolly
  - Joseph L'Estrange – bapt. 23 Sep 1850 (Baptism, **St. Michan Parish** (RC))
- William Henry L'Estrange & Jane Sheridan
  - William Henry L'Estrange – b. 6 Jul 1894, bapt. 11 Jul 1894 (Baptism, **Rathmines Parish** (RC))
  - Mary Gertrude L'Estrange – b. 24 May 1896, bapt. 27 May 1896 (Baptism, **Rathmines Parish** (RC))

William Henry L'Estrange (father):

Residence - 20 Ashfield Road - July 11, 1894

May 27, 1896

- William Rose L'Estrange & Elizabeth L'Estrange
  - Henry L'Estrange – b. 14 Aug 1855, bapt. 19 Aug 1855 (Baptism, **Carlow Parish**)

William Rose L'Estrange (father):

Residence - Carlow Union - August 19, 1855

Individual Baptisms/Births

- Louisa L'Estrange – bapt. 29 Jun 1838 (Baptism, **St. Paul Parish**)

- Margaret Anne L'Estrange – bapt. 30 Nov 1847 (Baptism, **Clontarf Parish**)

- Unknown L'Estrange – bapt. Unclear (Baptism, **St. Werburgh Parish**)

Individual Burials

- A. B. L'Estrange – b. 1846, bur. 18 Feb 1846 (Burial, **St. Peter Parish**)

A. B. L'Estrange (deceased):

    Residence - Fitzwilliam Square - before February 18, 1846

    Age at Death - 3 weeks

- Anne L'Estrange – bur. 3 Mar 1798 (Burial, **St. James Parish**)

Anne L'Estrange (deceased):

    Residence - Ship Street - before March 3, 1798

- Cecilia L'Estrange – b. 1845, d. 14 Sep 1853, bur. 1853 (Burial, **St. Peter Parish**)

Cecilia L'Estrange (deceased):

    Residence - Brighton Terrace, Kingstown - September 14, 1853

    Age at Death - 8 years

- Esther L'Estrange – b. 1710, bur. 29 Jun 1795 (Burial, **St. Werburgh Parish**)

Esther L'Estrange (deceased):

    Residence - Hoey's Court - before June 29, 1795

    Age at Death - 85 years

L'Estrange Surname Ireland: 1600s to 1900s

- Fredeswide Dorothea L'Estrange – b. 1768, bur. 28 Jan 1850 (Burial, **St. Mary Parish**)

Fredeswide Dorothea L'Estrange (deceased):

    Residence - 27 Richmond Place - before January 28, 1850

    Age at Death - 82 years

- Henry L'Estrange – b. 1813, bur. 1 Nov 1839 (Burial, **St. Peter Parish**)

Henry L'Estrange (deceased):

    Residence - Fitzwilliam Square - before November 1, 1839

    Age at Death - 26 years

    Place of Burial - St. Peter's Cemetery

- Henry G. F. L'Estrange – b. Aug 1865, bur. 9 Nov 1865, bur. 13 Nov 1865 (Burial, **Irishtown Parish**)

Henry G. F. L'Estrange (deceased):

    Residence - Beggar's Bush, Irishtown - before November 13, 1865

    Age at Death - 4 months

- Isabel L'Estrange – b. 1786, d. 10 Nov 1843, bur. 1843 (Burial, **St. Peter Parish**)

Isabel L'Estrange (deceased):

    Residence - York Street - November 10, 1843

    Age at Death - 57 years

Hurst

- John L'Estrange – bur. 22 Jul 1752 (Burial, **St. Catherine Parish**)

- John L. L'Estrange – b. 1758, bur. 27 Jul 1808 (Burial, **St. Werburgh Parish**)

John L'Estrange (deceased):

    Occupation - Late Curate of St. Werburgh - before July 27, 1808

    Age at Death - 50 years

- Margaret L'Estrange – b. 1775, d. 7 Dec 1836, bur. 1836 (Burial, **St. Peter Parish**)

Margaret L'Estrange (deceased):

    Residence - Leeson Street - December 7, 1836

    Age at Death - 61 years

- Marshall L'Estrange – bur. 10 Jan 1716 (Burial, **St. Catherine Parish**)

Marshall L'Estrange (deceased):

    Age at Death - child

- Mary L'Estrange – bur. 15 Mar 1752 (Burial, **St. James Parish**)

Mary L'Estrange (deceased):

    Residence - Ormond Quay - before March 15, 1752

- Mary L'Estrange – b. 1762, bur. 3 Jul 1832 (Burial, **St. Audoen Parish**)

Mary L'Estrange (deceased):

    Relationship Status at Death - widow

L'Estrange Surname Ireland: 1600s to 1900s

Age at Death - 70 years

- Peter L'Estrange – bur. 17 Jun 1828 (Burial, **St. Paul Parish**)

- Samuel L'Estrange – b. 1783, d. 6 May 1818 (Burial, **St. Anne Parish**)

Samuel L'Estrange (deceased):

Age at Death - 35 years

- Sarah Georgina L'Estrange – b. 1830, bur. 19 Apr 1838 (Burial, **St. Peter Parish**)

Sarah Georgina L'Estrange (deceased):

Residence - Fitzwilliam Square - before April 19, 1838

Age at Death - 8 years

Place of Burial - St. Peter Cemetery

- Unknown L'Estrange (Child) – bur. 21 Mar 1798 (Burial, **St. Mary Parish**)

Unknown L'Estrange (Child) (deceased):

Residence - Great George Street - before March 21, 1798

Occupation - Esquire - before March 21, 1798

- Unknown L'Estrange (Child) – bur. 12 Oct 1798 (Burial, **St. Mary Parish**)

Unknown L'Estrange (Child) (deceased):

Residence - Henry Street - before October 12, 1798

Hurst

- Unknown L'Estrange (Mr.) – bur. 29 Oct 1796 (Burial, **St. Mary Parish**)

Unknown L'Estrange (Mr.) (deceased):

Residence - Drogheda Street - before October 29, 1796

- Unknown L'Estrange (Mrs.) – bur. 14 Nov 1767 (Burial, **St. Mary Parish**)

Unknown L'Estrange (Mrs.) (Deceased):

Residence - Bolton Street, Chancel Vault - before November 14, 1767

- Usher L'Estrange – d. 3 Jan 1831, bur. 1831 (Burial, **St. James Parish**)

Usher L'Estrange (deceased):

Residence - Dolphin's Barn - January 3, 1831

- William L'Estrange – bur. 28 Jan 1828 (Burial, **St. Nicholas Without Parish**)

William L'Estrange (deceased):

Residence - Bull Alley - before January 28, 1828

Individual Marriages

- Adelaide L'Estrange & Matthew James

  o Mary Georgina James – b. 18 Apr 1867, bapt. 22 Apr 1867 (Baptism, **SS. Michael & John Parish (RC)**)

  o Thomas Joseph James – b. 27 Feb 1870, bapt. 7 Mar 1870 (Baptism, **St. Nicholas Parish** (RC))

  o Julie Teresa James, b. 20 Oct 1871, bapt. 30 Oct 1871 (Baptism, **SS. Michael & John Parish** (RC)) & Robert Crooke – 28 Feb 1897 (Marriage, **St. Mary, Pro Cathedral Parish** (RC))

Julie Teresa James (daughter):

    Residence - 6 Summer Hill - February 28, 1897

Robert Crooke, son of John Crooke & Joan Fitzgerald (son-in-law):

    Residence - 5 Lower Dominick Street - February 28, 1897

Wedding Witnesses:

Peter Brown & Mary James

    o Mary Anne James – b. 22 Oct 1876, bapt. 30 Oct 1876 (Baptism, **St. Nicholas Parish** (RC))

    o Edward Matthew James – b. 6 Aug 1879, bapt. 18 Aug 1879 (Baptism, **St. Nicholas Parish** (RC))

    o William James – b. 1882, bapt. 1882 (Baptism, **St. Andrew Parish** (RC))

Matthew James (father):

    Residence - 16 Wood Quay - April 22, 1867

        17 Great Ship Street - March 7, 1870

Hurst

- Anne L'Estrange & Gulielmo Payne

  o Mary Payne – bapt. 19 Aug 1832 (Baptism, **St. Michan Parish (RC)**)

- Anne L'Estrange & James Hoolahan

  o James Hoolahan – b. 7 Nov 1857, bapt. 16 Nov 1857 (Baptism, **St. Mary, Pro Cathedral Parish (RC)**)

  o Patrick James Hoolahan – b. 29 Oct 1862, bapt. 12 Nov 1862 (Baptism, **St. Mary, Pro Cathedral Parish (RC)**)

  o Julie Ellen Hoolahan – b. 29 Oct 1862, bapt. 12 Nov 1862 (Baptism, **St. Mary, Pro Cathedral Parish (RC)**)

James Hoolahan (father):

Residence - 18 Little Mary Street - November 16, 1857

10 Little Mary Street - November 12, 1862

- Anne L'Estrange & Owen Clarke – 19 May 1780 (Marriage, **St. Michan Parish (RC)**)

Wedding Witnesses:

John Clarke, Elizabeth Clarke, Mary Murphy, & Catherine Tyrell

L'Estrange Surname Ireland: 1600s to 1900s

- Arabella L'Estrange & Charles Seaton – 5 May 1792 (Marriage, **St. Thomas Parish**)

- Bridget L'Estrange & Peter McGarry – 14 Jan 1840 (Baptism, **St. Catherine Parish** (RC))

    o Elizabeth McGarry – bapt. Nov 1843 (Baptism, **St. James Parish** (RC))

    o John McGarry – bapt. 7 Nov 1844 (Baptism, **St. James Parish** (RC))

    o Margaret McGarry – bapt. 6 Oct 1847 (Baptism, **St. Nicholas Parish** (RC))

    o Bridget McGarry – bapt. 20 Sep 1851 (Baptism, **St. Catherine Parish** (RC))

    o Thomas McGary – b. 18 Feb 1857, bapt. Feb 1857 (Baptism, **St. Catherine Parish** (RC))

Peter McGarry (father):

Residence - 4 Hanbury Lane - February 1857

Wedding Witnesses:

Margaret Glynn & Margaret Fitzpatrick

- Catherine L'Estrange & George Witton

    o Elizabeth Catherine Witton – b. 3 Jan 1892, bapt. 4 Jan 1892 (Baptism, **St. Mary, Pro Cathedral Parish** (RC))

George Witton (father):

Residence - 107 Lower Tyrone Street - January 4, 1892

- Catherine L'Estrange & James Hannon – 23 Jan 1820 (Marriage, **St. Catherine Parish** (RC))

Wedding Witnesses:

Robert Byrne & Hannah Carroll

- Catherine L'Estrange & James Rooney

    o William Rooney – bapt. 1 Dec 1812 (Baptism, **SS. Michael & John Parish** (RC))

Hurst

- Catherine L'Estrange & Philip Hughes

  - Mary Hughes – b. 1851, bapt. 1851 (Baptism, **Chapelizod Parish** (RC))

  - John Hughes – b. 1853, bapt. 1853 (Baptism, **Chapelizod Parish** (RC))

Philip Hughes (father):

Residence - Chapelizod - 1851

Park - 1853

- Elizabeth L'Estrange & George Fagan – 22 Nov 1838 (Marriage, **St. George Parish**)

Signatures:

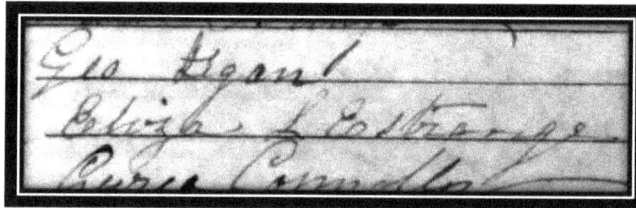

Elizabeth L'Estrange (wife):

Residence - No. 26 Nelson Street, St. George Parish - November 22, 1838

George Fagan (husband):

Residence - No. 5 Arran Quay, St. Michan Parish - November 22, 1838

Occupation - Merchant - November 22, 1838

Wedding Witnesses:

George Connolly & Patrick Fawler

L'Estrange Surname Ireland: 1600s to 1900s

Signatures:

- Elizabeth L'Estrange & John Costigan

  o Catherine Mary Costigan – b. 20 Jan 1895, bapt. 21 Jan 1895 (Baptism, **St. Agatha Parish** (RC))

  o John Patrick Costigan – b. 22 Mar 1899, bapt. 27 Mar 1899 (Baptism, **St. Mary, Pro Cathedral Parish** (RC))

John Costigan (father):

Residence - **5 Synnott Street - January 21, 1895**

51 Summer Hill - March 27, 1899

- Elizabeth L'Estrange & John Rourke

  o Daniel Rourke – bapt. 15 Jan 1826 (Baptism, **SS. Michael & John Parish** (RC))

- Elizabeth L'Estrange & Michael Murray

  o Matthew Murray– bapt. 25 Apr 1856 (Baptism, **St. Catherine Parish** (RC))

  o Mary Teresa Murray – b. 5 Sep 1858, bapt. 7 Sep 1858 (Baptism, **St. Catherine Parish** (RC))

  o Roseanne Murray – b. 20 Aug 1860, bapt. 21 Aug 1860 (Baptism, **St. Catherine Parish** (RC))

Michael Murray (father):

Residence - **117 Thomas Street - September 7, 1858**

123 Thomas Street - August 21, 1860

Hurst

- Elizabeth L'Estrange & Patrick Doyle – 17 Nov 1852 (Marriage, **St. Audoen Parish** (RC))

Wedding Witnesses:

Thomas Sarsfield & Elizabeth Lambe

- Elizabeth L'Estrange & Patrick Doyle – 14 Jun 1854 (Marriage, **St. Nicholas Parish** (RC))

Wedding Witnesses:

Edward Sherwood & Catherine King

- Elizabeth L'Estrange & Timothy Roach – 29 Apr 1805 (Marriage, **St. Andrew Parish** (RC))

Wedding Witnesses:

John Bartley & Eleanor Mack

- Elizabeth L'Estrange & William Broden – 18 Nov 1707 (Marriage, **St. John Parish**)

- Elizabeth Augusta L'Estrange & William Ledwich – 2 Mar 1835 (Marriage, **St. Mary Parish**)

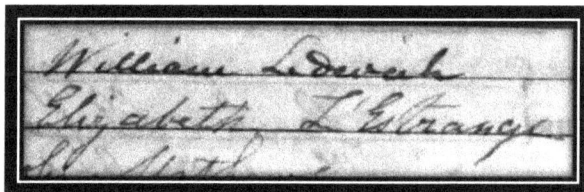

Signatures:

Elizabeth Augusta L'Estrange (wife):

    Residence - St. Mary Parish - March 2, 1835

William Ledwich (husband):

    Residence - St. Mary Parish - March 2, 1835

L'Estrange Surname Ireland: 1600s to 1900s

Wedding Witnesses:

John Mathews & Henry George Hughes

Signatures:

- Elizabeth L'Estrange & William Henry Johnson

  o Maude Johnson – b. 10 Jan 1888, bapt. 6 Feb 1888 (Baptism, **SS. Michael & John Parish** (RC))

William Henry Johnson (father):

Residence - 35 Parliament Street - February 6, 1888

- Esther L'Estrange & George Gifford

  o Elizabeth Gifford – b. 1 Jan 1863, bapt. 16 Jan 1863 (Baptism, **St. Nicholas Parish** (RC))

George Gifford (father):

Residence - 30 Chancery Lane - January 16, 1863

- Frances L'Estrange & Robert Walpole – 5 Jan 1758 (Marriage, **St. Mary Parish**)

Hurst

- Grace L'Estrange & Edmond William O'Mahony – 11 Sep 1851 (Marriage, **St. Anne Parish**) (Marriage, **St. Andrew Parish** (RC))

Signatures:

Grace L'Estrange (wife):

    Residence - 27 Molesworth Street - September 11, 1851

Edmond William O'Mahony (husband):

    Residence - 108 Lowere Gardiner Street - September 11, 1851

    Occupation - Barrister at Law - September 11, 1851

Wedding Witnesses:

John Vesey Forde, M. Louisa Armstrong, & Michael Gormley

Signatures:

L'Estrange Surname Ireland: 1600s to 1900s

- Jane L'Estrange & John Rourke

    o Gulielmo Patrick Rourke – b. 4 Mar 1867, bapt. 6 Mar 1867 (Baptism, **St. Mary, Pro Cathedral Parish (RC)**)

    o John Rourke & Mary Anne Campion – 14 Aug 1881 (Marriage, **St. Mary, Pro Cathedral Parish (RC)**)

John Rourke (son):

    Residence - 70 Montgomery Street - August 14, 1881

Mary Anne Campion, daughter of John Campion & Elizabeth McCann (daughter-in-law):

    Residence - 70 Montgomery Street - August 14, 1881

Wedding Witnesses:

James Haide & Esther Brennan

    o William Rourke & Rose Hayles – 8 Jul 1894 (Marriage, **St. Mary, Pro Cathedral Parish (RC)**)

William Rourke (son):

    Residence - 34 Upper Tyrone Street - July 8, 1894

Rose Hayles, daughter of John Hayles & Margaret Holly (daughter-in-law):

    Residence - 15 Upper Buckingham Street - July 8, 1894

Wedding Witnesses:

John Rourke & Anne Reilly

Hurst

- ○ Edward Rourke – b. 5 Sep 1876, bapt. 11 Sep 1876 (Baptism, **St. Mary, Pro Cathedral Parish (RC)**)

- ○ Mary Rourke – b. 29 May 1879, bapt. 4 Jun 1879 (Baptism, **St. Mary, Pro Cathedral Parish (RC)**)

John Rourke (father):

Residence - 4 Beaver Street - March 6, 1867

3 Rutland Place - September 11, 1876

15 Montgomery Street - June 4, 1879

- Louisa L'Estrange & George Callaghan

  - ○ Louisa Callaghan – bapt. Jun 1849 (Baptism, **Rathmines Parish (RC)**)

- Louisa L'Estrange & Peter Cavanagh – 3 Nov 1832 (Marriage, **St. Paul Parish**)

- Margaret L'Estrange & Albert McConnell

  - ○ Joseph A. McConnell – b. 23 Apr 1867, bapt. 30 Apr 1867 (Baptism, **Rathmines Parish (RC)**)

Albert McConnell (father):

Residence - Kingsland Park - April 30, 1867

- Margaret L'Estrange & Charles P. Baxter – 30 Jun 1875 (Marriage, **St. Mary Parish (RC)**)

Wedding Witnesses:

Edward P. Lanphan & Emily Willis

L'Estrange Surname Ireland: 1600s to 1900s

- Margaret L'Estrange & Francis Fitzpatrick

  o John Fitzpatrick – bapt. 13 Oct 1829 (Baptism, **St. Nicholas Parish** (RC))

  o Richard Fitzpatrick – bapt. 2 Aug 1832 (Baptism, **St. Nicholas Parish** (RC))

  o Catherine Fitzpatrick – bapt. 1835 (Baptism, **St. Catherine Parish** (RC))

- Margaret L'Estrange & Frederick Vickery

  o John J. Vickery – b. 15 Aug 1873, bapt. 24 Aug 1873 (Baptism, **Rathmines Parish** (RC))

Frederick Vickery (father):

Residence - Portobello Barracks - August 24, 1873

- Margaret L'Estrange & George Doogan

  o Mary Doogan – bapt. 12 Apr 1836 (Baptism, **St. James Parish** (RC))

- Margaret L'Estrange & John Corbett – 23 Jan 1813 (Marriage, **St. James Parish**)

- Margaret L'Estrange & Thomas McNally

  o Mary McNally & John Kavanagh – 13 Sep 1867 (Marriage, **St. Lawrence Parish** (RC))

Mary McNally (daughter):

Residence - 3 Connolly Cottages, Nixon Street - September 13, 1867

John Kavanagh, son of Thomas Kavanagh & Anne Guilfoyle (daughter-in-law):

Residence - 3 Connolly Cottages, Nixon Street - September 13, 1867

Wedding Witnesses:

Patrick Higgins & Margaret McNally

Hurst

- Margaret L'Estrange & Thomas Northon – 16 Mar 1759 (Marriage, **St. Audoen Parish**)

- Mary L'Estrange & Edward Gaffney – 17 Jan 1850 (Marriage, **St. Andrew Parish** (RC))

Wedding Witnesses:

Richard Thornton & Rosetta Wade

- Mary L'Estrange & James Russell

  o Ellen Russell – b. 23 Mar 1890, bapt. 28 Mar 1890 (Baptism, **St. Mary, Pro Cathedral Parish** (RC))

  o Patrick John Russell – b. 1 Jan 1892, bapt. 4 Jan 1892 (Baptism, **St. Mary, Pro Cathedral Parish** (RC))

  o John Angelo Russell – b. 13 Oct 1893, bapt. 18 Oct 1893 (Baptism, **St. Mary, Pro Cathedral Parish** (RC))

James Russell (father):

Residence - 41 Lower Buckingham Street - March 28, 1890

January 4, 1892

October 18, 1893

- Mary L'Estrange & John Kavanagh

  o William Kavanagh – b. 5 Feb 1866, bapt. 16 Feb 1866 (Baptism, **St. Nicholas Parish** (RC))

John Kavanagh (father):

Residence - 3 Bride Street - February 16, 1866

L'Estrange Surname Ireland: 1600s to 1900s

- Mary L'Estrange & Meade Swift – 29 Aug 1800 (Marriage, **St. Bride Parish**)

- Mary L'Estrange & Michael Walsh – 29 Dec 1835 (Marriage, **St. James Parish** (RC))

  - William Walsh – bapt. 22 Apr 1836 (Baptism, **St. James Parish** (RC))

  - Michael Walsh – bapt. 22 Dec 1837 (Baptism, **St. Catherine Parish** (RC))

  - John Walsh – bapt. 8 Oct 1839 (Baptism, **St. Catherine Parish** (RC))

  - Mary Walsh – bapt. 9 Sep 1841 (Baptism, **St. James Parish** (RC))

  - Patrick Walsh – bapt. 6 May 1844 (Baptism, **St. James Parish** (RC))

  - Mary Elizabeth Walsh – bapt. 8 May 1846 (Baptism, **St. James Parish** (RC))

  - Elizabeth Walsh – bapt. 27 Aug 1847 (Baptism, **St. Catherine Parish** (RC))

Wedding Witnesses:

Gregory Duggan & Thomas L'Estrange

- Mary L'Estrange & Swift Meade – 29 Jun 1800 (Marriage, **St. Werburgh Parish**)

- Mary L'Estrange & Terence McManus

  - Hester McManus – bapt. 12 Nov 1811 (Baptism, **Schull East Parish** (RC))

- Mary L'Estrange & Thomas Gee – 14 Dec 1817 (Marriage, **St. Werburgh Parish**)

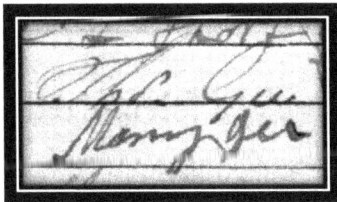

Signatures:

Mary L'Estrange (wife):

Residence - **St. Werburgh Parish** - December 14, 1817

Hurst

Thomas Gee (husband):

Residence - St. Werburgh Parish - December 14, 1817

Wedding Witnesses:

Thomas Madden & Catherine Madden

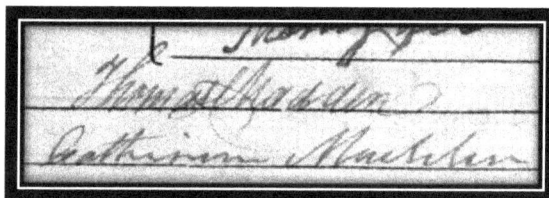

Signatures:

- Mary L'Estrange & William Courtenay

  o Elizabeth Mary Courtenay – b. 26 Apr 1900, bapt. 1 May 1900 (Baptism, Harrington Street Parish (RC))

William Courtenay (father):

Residence - 4 Bonney's Lane - May 1, 1900

- Mary Teresa L'Estrange & James O'Neill – 12 Apr 1812 (Marriage, St. Andrew Parish (RC))

Wedding Witnesses:

Henry O'Neill & Patrick O'Brien

- Rachel L'Estrange & John Kavanagh – 29 Jul 1844 (Marriage, St. Peter Parish)

  o Patrick Kavanagh – bapt. 28 Mar 1845 (Baptism, Rathmines Parish (RC))

  o Susan Kavanagh – bapt. 3 May 1846 (Baptism, Rathmines Parish (RC))

  o John Kavanagh & Mary McNulty – 21 Sep 1882 (Marriage, St. Mary, Pro Cathedral Parish (RC))

L'Estrange Surname Ireland: 1600s to 1900s

John Kavanagh (son):

    Residence - Dalkey - September 21, 1882

Mary McNulty, daughter of Peter McNulty & Elizabeth Brady (daughter-in-law):

    Residence - Ratoath - September 21, 1882

Wedding Witnesses:

Thomas Kavanagh & Alice McNulty

Rachel L'Estrange (mother):

    Residence - 18 Lower Kevin Street - July 29, 1844

John Kavanagh (father):

    Residence - 18 Lower Kevin Street - July 29, 1844

Wedding Witnesses:

Michael Donahue & Mary Donahue

- Roseanne L'Estrange & Michael O'Connor
  - Michael O'Connor – b. 29 Sep 1891, bapt. 2 Oct 1891 (Baptism, **St. Agatha Parish (RC)**)

Michael O'Connor (father):

    Residence - 4 Annesley Place - October 2, 1891

- Sarah L'Estrange & John Smith
  - Patrick Smith – bapt. 20 Mar 1837 (Baptism, **St. Nicholas Parish (RC)**)
  - Michael Smith – bapt. 8 Oct 1838 (Baptism, **St. James Parish (RC)**)

Hurst

- Sarah L'Estrange & Michael Cummins

  o John Cummins – bapt. 16 Jun 1834 (Baptism, **St. Nicholas Parish (RC)**)

- Sarah Isabel L'Estrange & Henry George Hughes – 24 Apr 1835 (Marriage, **St. Mary Parish**)

Signature:

Signatures (Marriage):

Sarah Isabel L'Estrange (wife):

Residence - St. Mary Parish - April 24, 1835

Henry George Hughes (husband):

Residence - St. Mary Parish - April 24, 1835

Wedding Witness:

Francis L'Estrange

Signature:

Name Variations

Includes Latin and Abbreviated forms of names found in the original documents.

Abigail = Abigale, Abigall

Anne = Ann, Anna, Annae

Bartholomew = Barth, Bartholmeus, Bartholomeo

Bridget = Birgis, Brigid, Brigida, Bridgit

Catherine = Catharine, Catharina, Catharinae, Catherina, Cath, Catha, Cathae, Cathe, Cathn, Kate

Charles = Carolus, Charls, Chas

Christopher = Christoph

Daniel = Danielem, Danielis

Edmund = Edmond

Edward = Ed, Edwd

Eleanor = Eleo, Eleonora, Elinor, Ellenor

Elizabeth = Betty, Elisa, Elisabeth, Eliz, Eliza, Elizab, Elizh, Elizth

Ellen = Elena, Ellena

Emily = Emilia

Esther = Essie, Ester

Francis = Fransicum

George = Geo, Georg, Georgius

Grace = Gratiae

Gulielmo = Guil, Guillelmi, Gulielmum, Guillelmus, Gulmi

Helen = Helena

L'Estrange Surname Ireland: 1600s to 1900s

Honor = Hanora, Honora

James = Jacobi, Jacobus, Jas

Jane = Joanna

Jeanne = Jeannae, Joannae

Joan = Johanna, Joney

John = Jno, Joannem, Joannes, Johannis

Joseph = Jos

Juliana = Julian

Leticia = Letitia, Lettice, Letticia

Lewis = Louis

Luke = Lucas

Margaret = Margarita, Margaritae, Margeret, Marget, Margt

Martha = Marthae

Mary = Maria, My

Mary Anne = Marianna, Marianne, Maryanne

Michael = Michaelis, Michl

Patrick = Pat, Patt, Patk, Patricii, Patricius

Peter = Petri

Richard = Ricardi, Ricardus, Rich, Richd

Robert = Roberti

Rose = Rosa, Rosse

Thomas = Thom, Thomae, Thoms, Thos, Ths

Timothy = Timotheus, Timy

William = Wil, Will, Willm, Wm

Notes

Notes

Notes

Notes

Notes

Notes

Index

Hurst

Hurst

L'Estrange Surname Ireland: 1600s to 1900s

L'Estrange Surname Ireland: 1600s to 1900s

Hurst

Hurst

About The Author

Donovan Hurst graduated from San Diego State University with a Bachelor of Arts in the major field of studies of History and a minor in the field of studies of Anthropology. He is a current member of The General Society of Mayflower Descendants and has been conducting genealogical research for over 10 years tracing back his ancestors to their ancestral homelands in Denmark, England, France, Germany, Ireland, Norway, and Scotland.

www.ingramcontent.com/pod-product-compliance
Lightning Source LLC
Chambersburg PA
CBHW081419270326
41931CB00015B/3329